75
FSG

Praise for **Music for the Dead and Resurrected**

"The voice of Valzhyna Mort is a miraculous reminder that words can do many things—they can dance, can bask in irony, can praise love, but they can also tell the truth. These poems are not only moving, they do the most elementary work of human language. They elevate the miserable, the barbarian, the numb, to the level of universal idioms of wisdom and grace."

—**Adam Zagajewski**, author of *Asymmetry*

"Her memory is incurable, and her imagination is anguished, because the small country she comes from is beauty and sorrow. Boldly, Valzhyna Mort stands out in the Belarusian poetic tradition. Reading her work, one feels that she has come to us from the whole earth."

—**Svetlana Alexievich**, Nobel laureate in literature

"Mort refutes the expected wistfulness of elegy in the way her poems speak so urgently, while also exhibiting a peacefulness threatened and a naturalness made dark . . . Her lines are gasping and anguished, but tempered with an inquisitive, tender pragmatism that steadies the tone of *Music*."

—**Julia Harrison**, *The Sewanee Review*

"In Valzhyna Mort's gorgeous *Music for the Dead and Resurrected*, images are often quirky and appealingly askew—a 'purse opened like a screaming mouth' and 'A bone is a key to my motherland [Minsk].' Mort writes: 'Among my people, only the dead / have human faces.'

What happens to the living then? The living, with their empty faces, must reckon with history and memory, 'the joy / of a deactivated face, / vacated face.' The living ask in a refrain, 'where am I from?' Mort answers back: language."

—Victoria Chang, *Oprah Daily*

"In the liminal space between language and silence, at dizzying imaginative speed, Mort transmutes her third language, English, into something resembling a fourth: the language of all that has been kept from consciousness concerning the century past. Her lyric art in contemporary English is astonishing, and glimmering beneath it is something not often encountered: the sensibility of another world, arriving to inform our perilous present. *Music for the Dead and Resurrected* is fiercely original and a tour de force."

—Carolyn Forché, author of *In the Lateness of the World*

Music for the Dead

and Resurrected

Also by Valzhyna Mort   *Collected Body* * *Factory of Tears*

Music for the Dead

and Resurrected

Valzhyna Mort

FARRAR STRAUS GIROUX / NEW YORK

Farrar, Straus and Giroux
120 Broadway, New York 10271

Printed in the United States of America
Published in 2020 by Farrar, Straus and Giroux
First paperback edition, 2021

The Library of Congress has cataloged the hardcover edition as follows:
Names: Mort, Valzhyna, 1981– author.
Title: Music for the dead and resurrected / Valzhyna Mort.
Description: First edition. | New York : Farrar, Straus and Giroux, 2020.
Identifiers: LCCN 2020026937 | ISBN 9780374252069 (hardcover)
Subjects: LCGFT: Poetry.
Classification: LCC PS3613.O778625 M87 2020 | DDC 811/.6—dc23
LC record available at https://lccn.loc.gov/2020026937

Paperback ISBN: 978-0-374-60324-3

Designed by Crisis

Our books may be purchased in bulk for promotional,
educational, or business use. Please contact your local
bookseller or the Macmillan Corporate and Premium
Sales Department at 1-800-221-7945, extension 5442, or
by e-mail at MacmillanSpecialMarkets@macmillan.com.

www.fsgbooks.com
www.twitter.com/fsgbooks
www.facebook.com/fsgbooks

10 9 8 7 6 5 4 3 2 1

for Korah

Contents

Music for the Dead and Resurrected

To Antigone, a Dispatch

allegro *for shooing off the police*
adagio *for washing the body*
scherzo *for soft laughter and tears*
rondo *for covering the body with good earth*

Antigone, dead siblings
are set.
As for the living—
pick me for a sister.

I, too, love a proper funeral.
Drag, Dig and Sisters' Pop-Up Burial.

Landlady,
I make the rounds of graves
keeping up
my family's
top-notch properties.

On a torture instrument
called an accordion
I stretch my bones
into fingers of a witch.

My guts have been emptied
like bellows
for the best sound.

Once we settle your brother,
I'll show you forests
of the unburied dead.

We'll clean the way only two sisters
can clean a house:

no bones scattered like dirty socks,
no ashes at the bottom of kneecaps.

Why bicker with husbands about dishes
when we've got
mountains of skulls to shine?

Labor and retribution we'll share, not girlie secrets.

Brought up by dolls and monuments,
I have the bearings
of a horse and a bitch,
I'm cement in tears.

You can spot my graves from afar,
marble like newborn skin.

Here, history comes to an end
like a movie
with rolling credits of headstones,
with nameless credits of mass graves.

Every ditch, every hill is suspect.

Pick me for a sister, Antigone.
In this suspicious land
I have a bright shovel of a face.

Bus Stops: Ars Poetica

Not books, but
a street opened my mouth like a doctor's spatula.

One by one, streets introduced themselves
with the names of national
murderers.

In the State Archives, covers
hardened like scabs
over the ledgers.

*

Inside a tiny apartment
I built myself

        into a separate room.

*

Inside a tiny apartment
I built myself

        into a separate room,
peopled it

        with the Calibans
of plans for the future.

Future that runs on the schedule of public buses,
         from the zoo to the circus,
         what future,
what is your alibi for these ledgers, these streets, this
    apartment, future?

         *

In the purse that held—
         through seven wars—
              the birth certificates
of the dead, my grandmother
hid—from me—
chocolates. The purse opened like a screaming mouth.

         *

The purse opened like a screaming mouth.
Its two shiny buckles watched me
through doors, through walls, through jazz.

Who has taught you to be a frightening face, purse?
I kiss your buckles, I swear myself your subject.

         *

August. Apples. I have nobody.
August. For me, a ripe apple is a brother.

For me, a four-legged table is a pet.

*

In the temple of Supermarket
I stand
like a candle

in the line to the priestesses who preserve
the knowledge of sausage prices, the virginity
of milk cartons. My future, small
change.

*

Future that runs on the schedule of public buses.
Streets introduce themselves
with the names
of national murderers. I build myself
into a separate room,
where memory,
the illegal migrant in time, cleans up
after imagination.

*

Bus stops:
my future, an empty seat.

*

In a room where memory strips the beds—
linens that hardened like scabs
on the mattresses—I kiss

little apples—my brothers—I kiss the buckles
that watch us through walls,
through years,
through jazz,
chocolates from a purse that held—through seven wars—
the birth certificates of the dead!

Hold me, brother-apple.

Genesis

I've always preferred Cain.

His angry
loneliness, his
lack of mother's
love, his Christian
sarcasm: "Am I
my brother's keeper?"
asks his brother's murderer.

Aren't we indeed
the keepers of our dead?

Let me start again:

I prefer apples that roll
far from the tree.

Dry like a twig
is umbilical cord, tucked between legs.

How did they cut it, Cain? With

a stone?

Under Criminal Record
write, "Mother, home."
Under Weapon
write, "Mother, home."

An Attempt at Genealogy

I

Where am I from?

In black basilicas
dragged incessantly
down a cross
is a man
who here resembles
a dress
       snatched from a hanger,
there: thick clouds of muscles—
                      an overcast body—
embodied weather
of one hardly known country.

(A country where I am from?)

Dragging him,
they stick their hands under his armpits.
How cozy their hands are
                 in such a warm place!

Through a cut in his chest
Eve watches
with her one bloody eye.

A cut in the chest—a red eyelash!

But
where am I from?

2

Yes, a man
resembles
a dress
          snatched from a hanger.

Inside black
                    alphabet
dragged incessantly down
each letter
is a man.

3

To a telephone in a long hallway
as if to a well for water.
(Well, where am I from?)

Neither mama's
nor papa's
my round face
takes after
a rotary phone:

A rotary phone is my gene pool.
My body rings as it runs
to put my head
on the strong shoulder of the receiver.

Blood is talking! Blood's connection is weak.
Inside the receiver I hear a crackling
as if fire were calling.
Who is this?

It's me, fire receiver.

But where am I from?

4

Days of merciless snow in the kitchen window—
snow was deposited like fat under our skin.

How large we grew on those days!
So much time spent at the kitchen table

14

trying to decide where to put commas
in sentences about made-up lives,

yet no one bothered to tell us
that words, once uttered,
crowd in the brain as in a hospital lobby.

That time is supposed to heal
only because once
it was seen with a scalpel in its hands.

You've made a mistake, you'd say mysteriously,
pointing at lines written by a child. *Think*

of another word with the same root.
As if words can have roots.

As if words didn't come from darkness,
cat-in-the-bag words,
as if our human roots were already

known to us.

Here's *Grammar*, here's *Orthography*,
here's a paper rag, "Bread, milk, butter."
What roots? What morphology? What rules

of subjugation? How is it even possible

to make a mistake? Here's *Physics, Chemistry,*
Geometry with its atlas, now,

where are Vaclav's letters,

1946?

What to do about the etymology of us?

Our etymology?

1946 crowds my hospital lobby.

The face of a rotary phone,
the face of a clock,
the face of a radio on the wall—
these are my
round-faced
progenitors.
But Vaclav's face—

where?

(again a man
resembles
a dress snatched from a hanger)

And where are the letters? One
per week, in his best Sunday
handwriting?

Inside the receiver—fire.
(How cozy are my ears in such a warm place!)
But where am I from?

5

A postwar Minsk barracks—

                    the joy of a first apartment—
a coat, a jacket, a leather purse
fat with pills, but where are
the where-letters
from the where-face?

Evacuated face,
de-evacuated face,
sick-not-sick, stuck-through face,
vacuum face,
lab rat face.

This country was tested on Vaclav's face.
Now we can live in peace.

So,
where am I from?

A postwar city, barracks—
                              the joy
        of a deactivated face,
vacated face.

A face snatched from a hanger.
Absence as an inner organ.

6

In a village known for a large puddle
where all children fall between the two categories

of those who hurt living things
and those who hurt nonliving things,

in a village known
for being unknown
(where am I from?),
a graveyard around an old church,
the frightening alphabet
around the village,
an alphabet on gravestones,
marble letters under the moth-eaten snow.

Under the moth-eaten snow
my motherland has good bones.

7

My motherland rattles its bone-keys.
A bone is a key to my motherland.

8

My motherland rattles its bone-keys.
Eve watches with her one red eyelash.

Under the moth-eaten snow
my motherland has good bones.

In my motherland people kneel before wells.
In my motherland people pray to the crosses of flying birds.

A bone is a key to my people.

Among my people, only the dead
have human faces.

Still,
where am I from?

9 (whisper)

Women saints in berets of golden threads,
who are these at your feet, sitting like pets?

An angel with wings of a peacock,
an angel with a human face.
But
    who are these at your feet,
                sitting like pets?

Now, if you wear such golden berets,
if you tame children and angels,
if your white boneless fingers leaf through a book
while I gnaw
        on this wooden verse,

would you, holy women who wear golden berets,
braid the hairs on my tongue

                into a pig-tail.

10

A mouse-tail of a word for a word-loving rodent!
Inside my alphabet
dragged incessantly down

each frightening letter
is a man.

My frightening alphabet in his best Sunday
                              handwriting.

A letter addressed to lost letters,
phone-face, clock-face, radio-face—
                              face as an inner organ.

Where are Vaclav's letters
                    as an inner organ.

On the borderlines of my motherland
              —wet laundry claps in the wind like gunfire.

Have you heard of my motherland?

My motherland is a raw yolk inside a Fabergé egg.
This yolk is what gives gold its color.

This face is a fire-receiver.
This face is an inner organ.
A bone as a key to my people.

Where am I from?

II

The golden bones of my motherland are ringing!

12

Put your bones into braids of graves, woods.
Put your bones into braids of graves, ravines.
Put your bones into braids of graves, fields.
Put your bones into braids of graves, swamps.

Put your graves into braids of bones, mother.
Put your graves into braids of bones, moth.
Put your graves into braids of bones, ghost.
Put your graves into braids of bones, guest.

Braid your bones neatly.
Braid your bones bravely.
Finger-comb your bones
into neat braids
in our woods, ravines, fields, swamps.

Little Song for

a Pocketknife

Marya Abramovic,
your two braids, a railroad
on your chest.

A train runs up and down your braids.
Your grandson plays a string quartet
with a pocketknife
on the window glass.

Outside—ever-red pines.
The train claps, claps, claps, claps.

Marya Abramovic,
mouth at shoulder length!

Marya Abramovic,
are they braids or truck tracks?

Marya Abramovic bakes gray bread.

A moon rib lies
on the kitchen table.

Marya Abramovic,
make yourself a tiny Eve,

to ease your nights,
to make chickens laugh.

Washday

Amelia does her washing by the wall
so bare you'd think she shaved it.

The window's open, anyone can see.
Soap hisses. An air-raid warning rings
like a telephone from the future.
Her dress is nailed to the laundry line.

From this gray garment, that is either guarding
or attacking the house, three yards of darkness
fall across the floorboards. She stands inside,
as at the bottom of a river, her heart an octopus.

Her hands so big, next to them,
her head is a small o
          (the neighbors squint),

stuffed hungrily with stubborn hair.

Little Songs

Over these houses
like a dead man's hands
the roofs are folded.

*

"A train?" "Dogs
rattle chains."
Windowsills, snowed over
with weary flies.

*

Amelia drinks thick coffee.
Yanina shares utensils like playing cards.
Yuzefa, after loud, theatrical farewells,

is dead.

*

Yuzefa crunches members
of broken households, she budgets
children and relatives, subtracts the dead,
carries over the missing.
It is a math problem
she buries with herself.

*

All windows in bride-white, a step-
house with step-inhabitants,
born in this kitchen, back three times a day
to have a meal in the place of their birth.

Yet none is buried anywhere close.

*

Yanina shovels snow piles of flies.
Like a manly tear, a bird glides across the air.

*

Chains follow dogs as if chains were discharged
like slime.

*

Justice has turned out to be
more terrifying
than injustice.
Yanina falls like dust onto her bed.

*

To look healthy? Leave that
to animals.

Once a tank drives through a street here.
Like an elephant,
it waves its trunk
from right to left.
An elephant in our village!
Instead of hiding, women run to look.

*

Since then, many birds are shed
across the air.
The dents on cups gag many thirsty mouths.

What has been done to us is muddled with the fears
of what could have been done.

Our famous skills
in tank production
have been redirected
at students and journalists.

But under that roof, folded
like a dead man's hands over the house,
we still live.

*

But under that roof, folded
like a dead man's hands over the house,

we still live
carrying buckets between a tree and a beast.
And instead of evening prayers
I plead
with myself
to just leave you
be, my dear, my

undear Lord.

Rose Pandemic

In a chance encounter, a stranger who knew you during your Mordovian evacuation described the horrible hunger, and described you as a hungry boy who always carried a book.

I

On this table made from foreign trees
the bread of silence, unbroken.

Mute, a portrait of myself: I'm framed

into the back of the chair. And you are here,
yet not. Your bones in the womb of the grave,

yet not, a hungry boy with a book, in a mass burial
next to your twins-in-death. Your name,

which sounded foreign to them,
is changed for a Russian name
in an act of un-baptism.
Yet, not.

The bread sits on square wooden shoulders.

When you go hungry for months,
your heart is a red bone.

All I see when I open a book is your empty stomach.

    2

Sometimes your clear stomach is a magnifying lens.
With it, I search from page to page
for an old potato dug into the soil of print.

I go so mad I listen to the pages of books
wondering if you chewed on the roots of trees
turned this paper.

Into my stomach-size fist
I fold a raisin, a walnut, some sugar.
With this fist I knock the air out of air,
strike whatever's around.

About me: I often spent a whole day between parking lots
where cars resemble giant turtle shells abandoned by all of life.
From these turtle cemeteries

I watch hills: ophthalmic distortion,
red barns: ants on my eyeballs.

My doctor prescribed me drops of Lethe water.

Why do I speak to you?
Favorite grandchild of your favorite sister,
the more Lethe I put in my eyes, the closer I am to you.

Inside my Noah's Ark—ghosts ready to beget ghosts.

Do you know what a ghost looks like?
It looks like blood.

3

Sitting a breath away from you, I'm afraid
of my tongue's shadow moving in the corners
of my mouth.

I pulled this house over my head like a cast
to heal fractured sanity, thought to thought.

I silenced all past with the spell of a camera flash,
yet not.

If there'd be a sound between us,
let it be one that starts
with touch,
which is music.

Music which, over accordion keys,
unclenches the fist of ancestry,
loosens fingers into rose petals.

A family tree is not a tree but a rosebud,
petals tied together, mouths down.

4

You listened for the sound of an iron
gate squealing like slaughter
and licked
your lips. Then, silence
straightened its shoulders inside your nostrils.

You died on a hospital sheet bleached
and starched until it seemed to be made
out of ironed bones.

What does the family rose think about that,
when my pen stands on end like hair on this paper?

34

5

From one hospital-white key to the next,
I carry my dead in order to tuck them into
these shrouds woven from sound.

I bury them, properly, one by one,
inside the piano-key coffins.

I rush—I learned to rush from Earth!
Earth, a bladder full of dirt and snow.

Yet not.

New Year in Vishnyowka

(A LULLABY)

Snow glints and softens
a pig's slaughter.

Mama refuses another
drink, mama
agrees to another drink.

On the wall—a carpet with peonies,
their purple mouths

                suck me into sleep.

Small,

      I've been bedded.

                        Toasts

from across the wall,

                my lullabies.

Mama says no-no-no
to more drink.

My bed smells of valenky.
Without taking its eyes off me
a cat

licks its gray paw as if sharpening a knife.
Mama yells yes to another drink.

Mama's breasts are too big to fit into packed morning buses.
There's uncertainty
                         I would grow into a real person.
But on a certain day
in Vishnyowka,
a pig

is slaughtered, mama whispers yes
yes yes yes
to more drink,
I'm vanishing into the peonies' throats,
peonies smell of valenky,
                         of pig's blood
on the snow.

Clock's hands leave a strange ski track.

Psalm 18

*

I pray to the trees and language migrates down my legs like
    mute cattle.
I pray to the wooden meat that never left its roots.

I, too, am meat braided into a string of thought.
I pray to the trees:

luminescent in the dark garden
is the square star
of a window frame, my old bedroom.
Ghosts, my teachers!

*

In the branches of lindens—breathe, my ghosts,
(blood in my ears!),

in the lindens—cheekbones, elbows
of my dead—in these green mirrors.

*

How could it be that I'm from this Earth,
yet trees are also from this Earth?

A laundry line sagged under bedding among weightless trees,
yarrow and burdock, Bach's fugue, Bach's silence on our
wet clean sheets.

Behind glass—portraits of the dead.

Close the curtains—motionless, they watch.
Open the curtains—they tremble.

Close the curtains—speechless, they watch.
Open the curtains—they whisper.

Trees, curtains—tremble.
On them
the dead wipe this prayer off their tongues.

*

At dusk, like eyesight, mint and dill
tense their smell. On a light curtain

wind polishes its bones.
Two beds along one wall,
where, head to head, we sleep.

The grave of memory, grave
upon grave of memory: a train of coffin-wagons,
headfirst rushes, headfirst
rushes, rushes, train upon train
arrives in the earth.

At the next stop: my ghosts, come out, take a breath,
I'd be waiting there. I'd bring
fresh dog rose tea in our Chinese thermos.

Singer

A yolk of honey in a glass of cooling milk.
Bats playful like butterflies on power lines.
In all your stories blood hangs like braids

of drying onions. Our village is so small
it doesn't have its own graveyard. Our souls
are sapped in the sour water of the bogs.

Men die in wars, their bodies their graves.
And women burn in fire. When midsummer
brings thunderstorms, we cannot sleep

because our house is a wooden sieve,
and crescent lightning cut off our hair.
The bogs ablaze, we sit all night in fear.

I always thought that your old trophy Singer,
would hurry us away on its arched back.
I thought we'd hold on to its mane of threads

from loosened spools along its Arabian spine,
the same threads that were sown into my skirts,
my underthings, first bras. What smell

came from those threads you had so long
sewn in, pulled out, sewn back into the clothes
that held together men who'd fall apart

undressed. The same threads between my legs!
I lash them, and the Singer gallops!

And sky hangs from the lightning's thread.
As in that poem: on Berlin's Jaegerstrasse
Aryan whores are wearing shirts ripped off
the sliced chests of our girls. My Singer-Horsey,

does everything have to be like a poem?

Music Practice

In the intermission between
two wars
your father sang a song.

By the time

I heard this song, it had no music.

Patching the lyrics with mmm and
aaa (after the third war you got by
as a seamstress),
you lost the thread
of melody and pitch.

This song, my daily dose of radiation

or vaccination, without words
except for off-key mooing,
except for
low-key bleating, this song
limping
through the lump in the throat. (My dead,
always peeping-tomming,
always peck-pocketing my small girl brain.)

Should I go ahead and profess
that in the name
of that man who played any instrument thrown at him
—a cimbalom, a mandolin, a fiddle—
but ended up quickly killable
once thrown into a war
(not even a Great one at that)

I was drafted into music.

Because your sole memory of your father
was a man singing a tune in the gooseberry yard
to a toddler
                    who, later,
could remember neither words nor melody,
I had to learn Bach,
Brahms, Rachmaninov, Haydn,

                              on a red accordion,

I had to put in
over thirty-two thousand hours of music
practice
(not unlike the Nazis,

on your dainty wristwatch,
you meticulously kept track
of my every sitting

subtracted trips to the bathroom
                              carried out under your disapproving,
suspecting gaze).

I had neither ear nor voice for it
(neither did you, I would add,
since now you cannot contradict me).

What can a toddler, mouth full of gooseberries, understand
    about a song?
What could a tongue remember after loss and hunger?

If I didn't know how we are made, I'd say
you had no father at all.

His song sounds too improbable.

It goes mmm and aaa
without melody, without
music.

All there is to it
is your sad face

that goes mmm and aaa
to Bach, Brahms, Rachmaninov—

Gamma Rays

Cupid's arrow	a scissor's beak I've stuck into my thighs, thirty kilometers from Minsk, sunstruck.
The sun	Chernobyl radio station. Broadcasts its radiation; is always on. The sun speaks into the tulips' microphones.
Microphones	Viktsya sits by the cow's udder like in a recording studio.
Record	Yanina (blind) copies sheet music from my teacher's songbook, *Beethoven* (deaf) *for Accordion*, into my notebook.
Xerox	unavailable in the empire, prized like a spacecraft.
Musical staff (according to the **music teacher**)	not Yanina's kitchen shelves. Unacceptable to reshelve at liberty, to adjust music pitch like spices.

Music teacher	a beautiful woman, furious like Beethoven's hair.
Musical staff (according to Yanina)	rows of plank beds in the northern barracks. "Notes are the bodies, rounded and flattened by day's labor, either utterly dark or insanely empty inside. This is what makes music so poignant, so painful."
Notes, *also* (according to Yanina)	ladles.

Beethoven: "Music should strike fire from the heart of man, and bring tears from the eyes of woman."

Yanina to Beethoven: "So music is a family brawl?"

Notes (according to the music teacher)	ladles full of water Yanina dumps onto Beethoven's fire.

My heart   on fire   with fury
every time the music teacher slams
     Yanina's blind copying.

I despise and secretly envy Beethoven
for having nothing to do

                 with plank beds in the northern
                 barracks.

A daily source of Beethoven: "Chernobyl" radio station.
The joy of radioactive rains.

My mission: I combat gamma rays with music octaves.

Yanina tucks notes into the plank beds of music staff.
On one of them, she recognizes   her old husband.
Her blindness   blurs all features   into the ovals   of notes.

The cow chews ribgrass but there is no cow.

Birds shred the clouds   with their dull beaks.
The woods are thin
like soup.   Men live
only on photographs,
alone
      old women are old women.

They lock in dentures. They log
glasses onto hooked noses.   They hook
themselves into forklifting bras,

secure kerchiefs   with sailor's knots
and thus, protected more thoroughly than first responders,
they curse their hens and pigs as if they had
hens and pigs.

                    A rooster's call,
quick like a vaccine shot.
The scissor's beak is as far as a cupid's arrow gets here.

I fall in love with music she miscopies,
music she syncopates, mis-
carring and miscoping,
without a peep.

A Song for a Raised Voice
and a Screwdriver

Having climbed into my lap, the accordion
composes
its heavy breathing.

                Who
turned Gregor Samsa
into this black box?   The old man

who taught me to play accordion banged
a screwdriver on a school desk.
For what?
For a beat!

He wore thick glasses, with lenses yellowed like toenails.
Ex-soldier, he had war medals and no rhythm.

Stepanych, you banged the accordion buttons
like a man stuck in an elevator.

I limped
across the keys
following the promise of the screwdriver.

Listen to me now missing the beat as if dodging
rubber bullets, Stepanych, I'm your student

to the bone. Stepanych, I'm
a bone snatched
by the giant spider
of an accordion, stretching its leggy belts

                                        over my back.

"His strange heart beating next to mine" and yada yada.

I imagine you buried with that screwdriver
like with a scepter—an emperor,
Stepanych the Pitchless.

Your student places her accordion like an ancestral
altar
on an empty chair.

Children, we learned rhythm
from the piss-stained hiccup of elevators,
from the broken blinking of traffic lights.

I'm barricaded behind a sob.

Give me that screwdriver beat, Stepanych,
and I'll be off.

Baba Bronya

On Pravda Avenue, four women protect 60 square meters of our family pravda. In the apartment building that stretches for two bus stops, I am a test-child exposed to the burning reactor of my grandmother's memory. In the first decade of my life, I receive a full dose of her—your—pravda [truth] as a daily injection.

When, in the winter dark I complain about having to go to school, you bring up 1941: you have just finished fourth grade in a Minsk orphanage. The first day of war puts an end to your education. "What would have become of me if not for war?" It is impossible to imagine you as anything else but a pravda-teller of your life.

As I eat my lunch, you talk, with gusto, about hunger. When I complain about my unfashionable clothes, you laugh remembering your wedding—you borrowed a white robe from a nurse to wear as a wedding dress. When I beg for privacy, you ask: "Did I tell you about the day the Bolsheviks came to take the roof off our farmhouse?" Or worse: "Did I tell you about the house where my mother died right after sending my brothers and me to an orphanage?" "Did I tell you about how Uncle Kazik died?" "Did I tell you how the Soviets took my father twice, and since he did return after the first time, I didn't cry a bit when they took him the second time?"

(Later you did cry abundantly when Stalin died.)

You remember the names of all our dead relatives and know the distances between the burned-down villages. You remember childhood rhymes and the exact dates of non-consequential occurrences (a bee stung your great-uncle Leopold in the eye on July 11). But you never remember that you have already told me these stories before.

"Have I ever told you about my life?" you'd say at night from your bed.

Three of us share one bedroom: my sister, you and I. My parents sleep on a sofabed in the living room. I've never set foot inside our second bedroom.

When I feel unwell, you talk about your leg that doesn't bend in the knee. A stick instead of a leg! Right before the war you are scheduled for kneecap surgery, but the bombings cancel all plans and for five years the knee rots. It is a miracle that in the end the leg doesn't have to be amputated. In the first months after the war, waiting for the surgery, you sit in the garden of Aunt Viktya's house, when a soldier on his long way home stops by the fence. "Beautiful, would you pick me a flower?" he asks.

All your stories feature this moment—whether it is a story of hunger, bombing, exile, sickness or death—somebody always stops by to tell you how pretty you are.

Unable to walk by yourself, silently, you keep to your seat. Before leaving, the man says (in your most dramatic voice): "Your eyes will haunt my dreams."
"I was ashamed to reveal that I was an invalid," you explain, daily.

For me, your stories [pravdas] replace real life. These stories keep me inside them like a circle of fire. As I grow older, you make sure I stay chained to a listening chair with an accordion. You help fasten a large, red Weltmeister on my skinny shoulders like a stone sinker. I sit on the bottom of your stories with an accordion holding me down.

Have I told you about how much I live inside your pravdas and not Pravda Avenue?

Neighbors find out about my accordion before my parents do and bang on the wall with a shoe. In a small, stinky elevator, some neighbor often asks me if I am *that accordion girl* and stares at me silently all the way up.

Once, giving my best to another étude or waltz, out of a corner of my eye I notice a tall figure standing in the door of the living room. She is an old woman, much older than my grandmother, with distinct features on a clear face. She is a total stranger inside our apartment.

This woman is my grandmother's aunt, Branislava, Baba Bronya. It turns out that Baba Bronya has lived with us, in our 60 square meters, for all the seven years of my life, occupying the second bedroom. My grandmother takes food to her room and cleans after her. Neither of Bronya's sisters wants Bronya and so she's ended up with us, on Pravda Avenue.

Bronya's two sisters, Viktya and Yadzya, along with her nieces, all Yadzyas, Yaninas and Amelias, never forgive Aunt Bronya for having a good time during the war. In the pictures I find years later, Branislava stands surrounded by men in uniform, and seems about to go dancing or to have just returned from a dance.

Above all, Bronya is hated for never having children: when you do not have children, you do not have to see them die one after another during the war.

I marvel at your ability to account for the exact causes of deaths of various children in the extended family. You recite them like recipes: "Edzik, 3, meningitis; Yanaczak, 1, diarrhea; Boleska, 5, in a bombing."

"Let's not cry," you tell me. "Viktya cried until her dead children in their afterlife almost drowned in her tears." Why not, you are always reliable for casually dropping facts about the afterlife as if you could enter and exit the afterlife right from your kitchen.

Have I told you about how much I live inside your pravda and not Pravda Avenue?

When Baba Bronya, long-haired and square-shouldered, emerges to the music through the doorway, I am seven years old, and I scream my lungs out. I cannot move, the accordion pins me down to the chair. You run from the kitchen, stuff Aunt Bronya back into her room (our second bedroom!), and I enter my years of nightmares and utter terror of being by myself. I have to be walked from the bedroom to the bathroom and back. On my way from school, I cannot enter our building and stand waiting for you to notice me from the kitchen window, so you can walk me in.

In the best Belarusian tradition, my mother drags me to many witch doctors. An image: early spring, we arrive from the city of apartment blocks in a village where a witch doctor lives in a low log house; snow pus glistens in the black humus.

Black humus, snow pus and whispers of village witches only increase my paranoias.

Once, almost a teenager, I walk into a church seeking exorcism.

After Aunt Bronya dies, my parents buy their first proper bed and move into the second bedroom.
What is left of Aunt Bronya? A small stack of yellowed photographs where she stands, long-haired and square-shouldered, surrounded by men in uniform. Have I told you how much I live inside your pravda and not Pravda Avenue?

My nightmares stop when, at sixteen, I quit studying music.

Guest

Here, where I'm dying, in a white house by a blue harbor.
—Maxim Bakhdanovich

Come in, Maxim! This is Minsk
choked under a pillow of clouds.

Here you are: a statue in a heavy coat.
Here all monuments wear coats.

Not wool, but linden bark coats,
with bee-fur collars.

In their pockets monuments keep belts.
And under collars monuments have necks.

In winter, shadows insulate the walls.
Windows and cracks are plucked with shadows.
In museums, coats and nooses

on display. And water is pickle juice.

Come in, Maxim, apartment blocks
are wrapped in ammunition staircases,
and window-medals sparkle through the night.

Every building here is a kind of bust,

an elevator ascends like vomit.
For furniture there is a stump.
Come in, Maxim, come flying!

*

Sit on a stump.
Don't cast a shadow. Keep
your coat on. And please
come flying, a comet-
statue flying,
a comet-medal
to Minsk.

Self-Portrait with Madonna

on Pravda Avenue

Whose mouth did you take me right out from?

The mouth of the street
named after the mouthpiece
of propaganda.

Of the empire's fall
I heard on the radio
while waiting for a weather forecast.

Swings became guillotines.
In the fluorescent classroom
pubescent critics
presided over
            a teacher,
who wrote on the blackboard with a tiny piece
of a human bone.

In that starched light,
she blinded our acned faces
with Raphael's Madonna.

We knew her bleached skin
by the smell. Corridors, disinfected with chlorine daily
to cover the reek of urine and sweat.

Chlorine, opium of the pupils,
granted us purity, absolution of sins
for our grandfathers
whose heroic deeds
        festered under torn book covers.

Public buses dug through the dark like hormonal moles.
Her docile features didn't seem beautiful.
Like hush money,
she was handing the child a breast.

The breast formed a kind of courtyard between their bodies.

What was his suffering to us?
The child held on to the breast so as not to humpty-
dumpty into the classroom where chlorine
long ago replaced speech.

In tiny offices reeking of glue,
bureaucrats picked their teeth in search
of a proper certificate
to record this strange birth.

A shot of snow into the blood-thick dark,
swings become guillotines,
the city of iron and irony.

The empire fell, then the snow fell, then the mother
ripped her dress and produced a breast ripe with thirty
silver droplets of milk.

In this starched light, on Madonna's chest
the child already looked crucified,
the nailhead of the nipple next to his little fist.

The art teacher looked starved. She despised us,
as did the star as it stared down in judgment.

She said, "Go." Like a worm,
her thin mouth tried to bury itself under her skin as she spoke.

A city of iron and irony,
a nest of snow larvae, my city.
Each snow maggot I kiss.

The mouth of Pravda Avenue I kiss.
I kiss each radio announcer on the mouth,
I kiss each radio announcer on her iron mouth,

history waits as we kiss.

Ode to Branca

Bless a life in which I run up the stairs
with a pharmacy bag full of pills for Branca.

O medicinal currency! Branca's rented health!
My virginity, a small pink coin in my pocket.

Bless a city that hides its column-ribs
under a nurse-clean robe of snow pandemics.

If the sun appears inside its boneless sky,
the sky is diagnosed with a tumor.
                              There's no sea,

but the graveyards splash their granite waves
into the yellow strips of street light—
                              light with sand in its teeth!

Bus stops glow in the dark—cigarettes, cell phones—
like nativity scenes.
Buses chew on the asphalt.

*

Bless Branca's dirty kitchen! In its grease, we are preserved.

When bread fell off the table, we tossed it out.
We washed our hands after visiting family graves
and didn't kiss the water that ran down the drain,
we flipped the light switch
with an elbow. But when we found love
on a fly flap between
fat and blood of flies and mosquitoes,
we licked it, with the very backs of our tongues.

Branca's lost my hand but she pulls my tongue like a puppet
    string: a tongue is always a mother's
whether I hold it back or thrust it so deep in your throat
    that to come out it has to become a song.

Bless a sign from an old man's mouth—his single totem-
    tooth.

*

Bless a hallway between languages where my lips are stacked
on each other like logs in a forest cabin.

Bless apartment blocks hung like Afghani rugs.

Bless a dog that runs with a crescent bone in its teeth,
flowers that smell of blood—home.

Its coordinates:
a star-wet water bucket,
breasts that hang like two hands,
each tipped with a nipple-finger,
a gravestone lock on the horizon chain.

Here's a poem in which my lip-logs need to shut it.

*

If they tell you earth doesn't breathe,
tell them how in spring
a river glistens with the belt buckles of thawing corpses,
tell them
how branches reach like death's helpful hands.

Tell them about birds in silk cages,
German shepherds on heavy chains,
a well by each house.

Shut it, lip-logs.

*

Tell them, lip-logs.

You can drink water from any well
or jump in and drown yourself.
You can hang yourself from one of the garden branches
or pick a half-rotten apple.

Bless this landscape of choices, clear as a clear night.

Turnips and beets grow straight into the throats
of the dead.

*

Nowhere else would you know this clearly that trees
are not mute, but choked.
They wind their lament:
what we have seen with all the hundreds of our eyes!
What we have seen with each of our green eyes!
Take these twigs, tear our eyes off, poke them out.

Shut it, lip-logs.

I'm reading this page like a fortune-teller.
I'm reading these lines like the palm of a hand.
When I see silk, I promise silk.
When I see blood, I promise blood.

What has kept us alive? Our death songs.

How did we scare God
out of this place?

With things that God fears:
a tongue, tied with a black ribbon of verse,
a slice of bread used as a bookmark.

*

Bless a life in which, still a child, I give a salute
and the book of my armpit opens
showing my black letters already grown.

And the voice that has led me
into the minds of trains and city buses,
into the minds of meat and milk shops?

On Branca's closed eyelids I put
her snow-white pills.

Nocturne for a Moving Train

The trees I've glimpsed from the window
of a night train were
the saddest trees.

They seemed about to speak,
then—
                    vanished like soldiers.

The hostesses handed out starched linens for sleep.
Passengers bent over small icons
of sandwiches.

In a tall glass, a spoon mixed sugar into coffee
banging its silver face against the facets.

The window reflected back a figure
struggling with white sheets.

The posts with names of towns promised
a possibility of words
for what flew by.

In lit-up windows people seemed to move
as if performing surgery on tables.

Chestnut parks sighed the sighs of creatures
capable of speech.

Radiation, an etymology of soil

directed into the future, prepared
a thesis on the new origins of old roots,
on secret, disfiguring missions of misspellings,
on the shocking betrayal of apples,
on the uncompromised loyalty of cesium.

My childish voice, my hands, my feet—all my things that live
on the edges of me—
shhh now, the chestnut parks are about to speak.

But now they've vanished.

I was extracted from my apartment block,
chained to the earth with iron playgrounds,
where iron swings rose like oil wells,

I was extracted before I could dig a language
out of air
with my childish feet.

I was extracted by beaks—storks, cranes.

See the conductor punching out eyes
of sleeping passengers.
What is it about my face
that turns it into a document,
into a ticket stretched out by a neck?

Why does unfolding this starched bedding
feel like
        skinning someone invisible?
Why can't the spoons, head-down in glasses, stop screaming?

Shhh . . .

The chestnuts are about to speak.

State of Light: 1986

A girl, I sing in the boys' choir,
mine is a city defaced with light's acid,
among the amphitheaters
of boys' mouths,

                my body—
a slice of nothing.

Muse,

        with two tongues where wings should be,
I begin with music

              thrown onto meat scales

in the city of acid,

           light speaks with the thin lips of streets,
           the thick lips of avenues, strings of light
stretched in the doorways of milk and meat shops,
music

       thrown onto meat scales

by saleswomen defaced with light's acid
by saleswomen whose hands are square like picture frames,
our saleswomen

who never see themselves in the canvasses
of great masters,
have the most pictorial lips—
arches of finest architecture,
triumphant arches built for their language of contempt.

They despise our hunger—
a child's place is in a choir, not at the table!

They despise our money—
*children shouldn't touch money, money is the genitals of our
State!*

We fry light to the screams of light
and we live on light

in this innocent city defaced with light's acid
built not on bones—not on bones—not on bones—not on
bones.

Not one splinter of human bones in our earth!
We can lower our hands into our earth as into water!

And my history book is stuffed like sausage.

2

Verily, in Your image: I hover
in the glory   of fish shops,
in the chlorine   of classrooms.

In my stomach   is the midnight of bread,
the abyss   of cognac.

As a species I'm closest
to a screw
          that loosens regularly.

In a Rembrandt-black bathroom
a girl-child—illiterate—washes me,
left to right my illiterate child
crosses and underlines
with a soaked sponge
what You've made in Your image.

She wasn't born.
She stood up and threw me off her back
                    like the skin of an animal.

I know a word for this
                but don't ask me—
ask a cow, ask a dog.

Verily: except for Rembrandt's right cheek,
it is dark.

Having picked
a headful of vines, Caravaggio
honestly paints the dirt under his fingernails.

No, honest historians, this dirt does not mean decay.
Under the charred nails: orchard,
origin (and I'm a screw that loosens regularly).

In its uncharted dark—

women washing each other
in the light of their cheeks,
in the light of their knees.

To Ingeborg Bachmann in Rome

You are not the last woman.

You are not the last woman to burn in Rome,
Ingeborg.
Under high foreheads of apartments just off the beaten path
everything's polished: wooden furniture, silver, teeth, the past.
After three baths a day, after forty years
of exposing your lungs to open books,
you are in bandages.

Ingeborg in coma, in white
bandages—Ingeborg
is a princess-bride worthy of that burned poet
Giordano Bruno.

Stretched out, faceup on the balcony over via Giulia,
did you know there are balconies where no one can stretch,
where you'd have to tiptoe strategically among jars
of pickled mushrooms, crates
                                of potatoes,
liters of compote. Where language

is a dog on a chain of iron words,
where punishment

        is a hundred lashes of silence.

Apartment buildings stand somber. Ingeborg,

                could they know
that inside them people die and cry?

In the night, when the last women are getting home,
    shopping bags over the basilic vein as if after drawing
        blood,
women who weigh the worth of things

                on their brows,
and know the best polish for any damaged surface,

the sounds of things occupy the city of men:
the car door slams, bottles bang in recycling bins,
basilicas rattle with candles like restaurant kitchens.

After three baths a day, Ingeborg, after hours
stretched out faceup on the balcony,
after forty years of holding books up to your lungs,

you still smell of Austria. Your straight hair
falls like currency in a counting machine.
Books stuffed around the apartment fail to perform

like air fresheners,
Ingeborg.

The yellow bile
of Western Union in the dark streets, the sickly light of night
    trams
under the high foreheads of polished apartments,
somber as if they could know, as if they could smell.
Stop smelling the past, Ingeborg.

As the whip of silence rises, language tucks in its tail.
And there it goes:

the flaming sword of a streetlamp—
Adam is boarding a train—
Eve is biting her elbows.

Paradise has a tree that bears Eve's bitten
elbows, Ingeborg.

I embrace these words with my teeth as I lie faceup on the
    balcony
overlooking your Rome.

Ours is a history whose every tooth is crowned.

Silence bleeds us to language.
Silence beats language out of us.
Praise your silence, Ingeborg, your hole in the wall.

Praise polished apartments—orchards—bitten elbows.
And silence.

Poet's Biography

I picked your book from Sandeep's shelf,
the poet's biography read: "lives and teaches."
Though the book was fairly recent, it was no longer true.

I almost met you once—an almost meeting I remember clearly
because of my embarrassment:
I was having loud sex in a hotel room
while you stood knocking at the door wanting to give me your
    book.

Now the trains stand frozen in a winter storm,
and I pity the trains
as if they were shivering butterflies,
a whole herd of them, the last of their kind,
stuck in the snow England has never seen.

Sandeep is cooking dinner, you are dead, the lover's gone,
your book in my frostbitten hands.

Music for Girl's Voice and Bison

I

Winter in Rome.

Poplars,
straight and stripped,
like Marsyas.

The river's dark iris
circles
                blind piazzas.
Tosca and Traviata

drink sour coffee
through an orange-slice
                                cut out of their faces.
They are twins,

rescued by a kitchen table,
nursed   by gooseflesh of oranges.

Their feet tap on the tiles
                                like choking fish;
their heads ring.

A ringing from the stomach. A ringing
beast
whose upper body is your own, reader,
while whatever's below the waist
is my dream.

*

In 1521, while watching a bullfight in the Colosseum, Mikola
Husowski remarks that the scene reminds him of a hunt for a
wild bison—zoobrr—biggest of its kind, that lives in the
woods of Belaveža—a primordial forest where Husowski
himself was born to a family of Litvin pagans.

Immediately, Pope Leo X orders Husowski to write down, in
verse, a detailed description of a pagan hunt for the eastern
beast.

*

You run your mouth, Mikola, and bison run—
the shape of toothache, the size of foam.

What do your arrows catch?
Your breath,

Mikola,
amid cypress trees and temples that crawl upon hills
        on their spider-leg columns,
how could you,

Mikola, above the arena
where bulls' baleful eyes blind the spectators
like camera flashes,

remember
of all the innumerable beasts—
one, of our
Belarusian woods

zoobrr, ash-wild,
veins arm-thick,
lungs like two tablets of stone.

Zoobrr looks straight
into the Medusa face
of what's to come.

*

On Earth,
where all disease is cured by walking,
zoobrr walks out of the woods
looking to kill
his loneliness,

a sylvan angel of history,
a bison of melancholia,
a black van.

*

I was in Rome:

better stuck between ribs of a wild bison,
better in Moloch's stomach clenched in free fall,
than between marble veins
that pump stone blood
inside stone muscles.

How could you, Mikola,
il forestiere, son of a Litvin
forester, now in Rome,
amid cypress trees and persimmons,
amid poplars, straight
and stripped, like Marsyas,
Mikola,

from our woods that only conifers
get to escape—
tarred with honey they swim

    —strange fish—to shipyards

where, rootless, amnesiac,
they are built into ships
that cross an ocean like a street.

    *

Mikola, under the rim of a ship's board—
Medea's chewing gum.

     *

Our strange fish carrying strange cargo—
from the woods where people worship sun,
genitals and a red thread sucked into white linen—

Mikola of one truth, one story, one God.
(Why
would a woman with thirteen children pray
to one God?)

A pope with a predator's name
and habits
commissions you to capture,
in verse,
our beast

whose lungs are two gravestones, side by side.

The left stone slightly smaller, on top—
a heart, like a forgotten hat,

a cap of red melted snow.

     *

What's heavier than a bison?
A bison's stare.

A tree stands decorated with wreaths of hunters' guts.
Our guts, a tangle of a girl's hair.
A map of our woods, a tangle of a girl's hair.

                *

1500: Copernicus, in Rome, observes the eclipse of the Sun.
1543: later, yet independently of Aristarchus, Copernicus
    describes the Sun as the central fire.

Belaveža is frozen.
Belaveža is beat by the storms of hunts.
Belaveža's sun is boarded like a closed-down shop.
Zoobrr, central beast, central black, central dream
in the icy air,

—dirt and ice rise to cheer its hooves—

runs and, running, smashes his shit to nothing
so that shit never hits soil,
so that he won't be tracked.

This is us then: bison's untraceable shit, smashed to ashes.
Our history
is a closed-down shop.

                *

Belaveža is shared between Belarus and Poland, with a borderline running through the forest. For the sake of clarity, we'll be referring to this borderline as a threshold of pain.

Pain-proof, yet
by any small sound
wounded,
zoobrr digs into the thicket past the skeletons
of trees.

A crown of guts on a frozen bush.

Bison is our black box,
a Trojan zoobrr packed with murdered poets,
a sylvan angel of history,
a bison of melancholia,
a black van.

   *

Bison of decency, bison of burdock and dill,
bison of small countries, bison of rape,
bison of having no evidence,
bison of illusions of golden past,
a beast with a name for people without a name,
bison of hostages, bison of early snow,
bison of misspellings, bison of barley and truce,
bison of Caesar and cesium

a beast whose name we could breathe
into a tube
to check the level of fear in our blood.

Bison of mob law, bison of smashed
dishes, bison of drooping mallows
        behind houses, emptied
like stomachs
at the dawn of a century.

Trojan bison of history,
Zoobrr, forgotten by Adam,
Zoobrr, filed as *uncategorized* in the depth of woods.
A people, misspelled, underlined
in red, filed as *uncategorized* in the depth
of apartment blocks.

        *

November. Bison are mating.
The woods tremble
as if somebody slowly
moved across them
an invisible fiddle bow
of light.

        *

November, bison-shaped.

II

In Rome, I had a habit of taking books in my language, written by authors no one in the West ever reads, to a swimming pool at a local gym.

Perspiring Italian tile, neon-blue water, museum-like quiet, and a European (almost) nude standing, walking, preparing to jump.

In a changing room, where women, rotating like clockwork, dressed and undressed, I would open my book exposing the alphabet of my language, the inked gooseflesh of its unheard-of, perverted signs.

Sweat and chlorine, crunch of snacks in clogged ears—the changing room was a womb. My strange letters—chromosomes, viruses—multiplied in the warm, moist air.

*

The radiation of the unknown tongue.

*

Once,
on my way to the pool,
on a dark rainy street,
I walked into a large pile of leaves,
disturbing it with my boot.
A maimed raven walked out, large,
heavy-chested, its wing
hanging like a black cabbage leaf.

"You have disturbed me," she said,
as she limped, bison-shaped,
straight into traffic.

To change the direction of thought—break a bird's wing.
I broke its wing.

To fix a misspelled letter of your name—pluck a bird's eye.

   *

I have disturbed you, my bison-shaped heart.
At the intersection between vocal cords
and war chronicles stands a bleeding zoobrr.
At arm's length, a zoobrr, ringing.
At arm's length, zoobrr sings with the voices of my dead.
I carry my zoobrr inside me. Absence
of explanation or evidence is my survival trick.

Absence of my blood from your history books
is the reason why, in the fall, fog spreads itself on earth
in a silent protest.

Fog is the bison of history.

*

Wherever I land, I upset the balance of borders.
Something in my blood makes me drop on your ground as
    stone drops
into a full glass.
I arrive and, at once, borders spill.

"Reason for your visit?" "Hairy history, sir."
"Reason for your visit?" "Book delivery for a starving bison."
"Reason for your visit?" "The closing of the shop of history."
"Occupation?" "Absence from history books."
"Occupation?" "Naming things a tangle of hair."
"Do you have any luggage?" "Yes."
"What's in your luggage?"
Ringing.

*

Through a diamond fence,
Mikola, dead, offers me
a handful of blueberries.

It is a dream. He looks so well-fed.
Our home is a womb on a frozen bush.

*

To untangle hair—untangle fog.
To untangle fog—release rivers into piazzas.
To release rivers—cut bison's throat,

now watch blood rush.

But what is blood

when blood

is a tangle of hair.

Acknowledgments

I'm grateful to the editors of the following publications in which my poems have appeared, sometimes in earlier versions: *Poetry*, *Poetry International*, *Granta*, *The White Review*, *The New Yorker*, *Prairie Schooner*, *Freeman's*, Poem-a-Day from the Academy of American Poets, *Ambit*, *The Common*, and *The Los Angeles Review*. Each enthusiastic response to my work gave me a new sweep of confidence—thank you.

A special thank-you to Kwame Dawes and the *Prairie Schooner* for honoring me with the Glenna Luschei Prairie Schooner Award.

My deep gratitude to the Amy Clampitt Residency Program, which has provided me with a writing residency where lots of these poems were drafted.

I also thank my husband, Ishion Hutchinson, for taking me on a year-long stay in Rome: lots of these poems were finished on the Janiculum Hill.

To my readers Ilya Kaminsky and Sandeep Parmar: I love you two. Thank you for your friendship, support, and patience.

Thank you to my editor, Jonathan Galassi, and everybody at FSG.

This book is for my daughter, Korah.